Where We Live

Philippines

Donna Bailey and Anna Sproule

RSVP

**RAINTREE
STECK-VAUGHN**
PUBLISHERS
The Steck-Vaughn Company

Austin, Texas

Hello! My name is Meliza.
These are my friends Maria,
Anita, Jose, and Ramon.
We live in the Philippines.

We live in the mountains at Banaue, near
the town of Bontoc, on the island of Luzon.
There are about 7,000 islands in the Philippines.
Luzon is one of the biggest islands.

It is very hot in the Philippines.
Our house has bamboo walls which
let the air in and keep the house cool.

4

My dad is a rice farmer and our village
is surrounded by rice fields.
The fields are made from terraces
carved out of the hillside.
The terraces were made over 2,000 years
ago by the Ifugao people.

We plant the rice on the terraces
in December when the heavy rains of
the monsoon season are over.
Everybody in the village helps
plant the seedlings.

When the rice has been planted, we have
a special festival in the village.
Everybody wears the traditional costumes
of the Ifugao people.

The older men wear shell necklaces
and carry spears for the festival.

The women wear brightly colored skirts
that they weave in the village.
It often rains at this time of year,
so everyone carries an umbrella.

Ifugao women are famous for their weaving.
They make bright patterns in the cloth.

During the festival, the drummers beat out
rhythms for our special dances.
We dance and hope that the rice will grow well
to give us a good harvest.

Rice needs a lot of water to grow, so
we flood the hillside terraces with water.
The water is pumped up from the river below.

When the rice is ready, the fields
are drained and the rice is harvested.
The rice is cut by hand using special knives.
Then it is tied in bundles and left
to dry in the sun.

Later, the bundles are gathered up and taken to be threshed.
Threshing separates the kernels of rice from the straw.
The children search the fields to find any stalks that have been dropped.

After threshing, there is always
lots of straw left in piles around
the village.

People use the straw to make thatch roofs.
A thatch roof gives good shelter
from the hard rain that falls
during the rainy season.

During the dry season from March to May,
tourists come to Bontoc and Banaue.
They come to see the rice terraces
and to buy the things
we make in the village.

In the Philippines, tourists travel by bus
or by special cars called jeepneys.
Jeepneys are like small buses that
carry passengers.
They are usually decorated in bright colors.

The tourists come to the mountains
to watch the women of Bontoc
weave patterns in their cloth.
This woman has even made patterns
on her arms!

The weavers make skirts, bags, and clothes.
They sell these things to the tourists
from stands by the side of the road.

The tourists also buy shell necklaces
like those worn by the older men
in the village.

Manila is the capital city of the Philippines.

Once, I visited my aunt who lives there.

I rode in a jeepney from my small village to Manila.

During the trip, our jeepney driver had to stop

to let a farmer cross the road with his ducks.

The farmers on the lowland plain near Manila
grow rice, just like we do in the mountains.
This farmer has a water buffalo
to help him plow his fields.

The buffalo also pulls a homemade platform called a pahagad.
The farmer piles the pahagad with supplies and rides the buffalo back to his home.

On the plains, people grow
coconuts as well as rice.

The farmers plant the coconut seedlings in
the warm, wet soil where they grow well.
The seedlings soon grow into coconut palms.

The farmers sell their coconuts, pineapples,
bananas, and other fruit from stands
by the side of the road.

I was in Manila during the festival
called Flores de Mayo.
The festival is held at the end of May.
I watched this band practice their
music before the festival.

The festival is in honor of the Virgin Mary.
Young girls decorate the statue of
the Virgin with flowers.
Then the men carry the statue
from the church.

People from different churches join in
the procession with their statues.
Some people carry statues of saints
or bishops.

In the evening, there is another procession
by candlelight.
Many of the women wear white veils.
The statues of the Virgin often have blue cloaks.
Blue and white are the Virgin Mary's colors.

The Festival of Santacruzan is also held in May.
The girls dress up in their best clothes and
parade under arches of flowers.
One of the girls is chosen to be
Queen of the Festival.